30 DAYS TO A NEW YOU

Journal

Your guide to developing self-awareness, mastering discipline, and retraining your thoughts to the path of positivity.

CHAR NEWELL

Copyright © 2020 Char Newell

All rights reserved. This book or any portion thereof may not be reproduced or used in any manner whatsoever without the express written permission of the publisher except for the use of brief quotations in a book review.

ISBN: 978-0-578-72657-1 (hardcover)

Dear Life Warriors,

I am illuminated with hope that you are taking the necessary steps to transform your Life. Allow me to share just a small bit of my Life's story with you, so you'd understand the purpose behind this 30-day journaling technique.

My amazing transformational journey began in 2016 when I had the most horrible break up. Of course, it would take a breakup for me to go and find myself. Lol. I am glad I went through it because it worked! The reason why this breakup rocked my world to the core was because everything was actually fine. We were happy and I was in love for the first time in my life, so you can imagine when I somehow uttered the words "We should stop trying," and he agreed, I was SHOCKED. I felt the words coming out my mouth, I wanted to stop it, but it was too late. He hung up and I was left with confusion. I had to ask myself, "Why are you so afraid to love and be loved?" This, my friend, is what sent me soul searching to discover the real me. I was immediately possessed with a deep burning desire to be at peace with everything that has happened to me in life.

This 30-day experience is really only the beginning of a lifelong process. Please don't expect yourself to be completely changed in 30 days, but this is the start of having a healthy mind. Becoming self-aware is key to understanding who you really are, and this challenge will have you address those negative emotions that have taken residence in your mind. This I can guarantee, your mind will never be the same after 30 days!

Good Luck, and please remember this, when you start to go into battle with your mind, it will go into battle with you. In the first 5 days, you will observe that the attacks will come more frequently and the blows will be harder to bear.

But, what do we say to a TOXIC MIND? NOT TODAY!!!

With Love,

Char Newell
Certified Master Life Coach

Please read these instructions before you begin

Important: You must be consistent for the 30 consecutive days, or you will not accomplish the goal. If you miss a day, you must start over again at day 1 until you are successful in completing the 30 days.

The Goal:

Develop Self-Awareness
Master discipline
Train your thoughts to be more positive.

Morning Routine: *Must be completed before you start your workday or leave the house.*

- Pray or repeat, "I am thankful for this beautiful day."
- Listen to a motivational message (10-30 mins long)
- Repeat a minimum of 3 positive affirmations over your life or set intentions for the day
  - *Examples- "This is going to be an amazing day," "I will complete everything on my to-do list," all my encounters today will deliver feel-good moments."*

- **Bonus 1**: play relaxing, soothing, spa music while you shower or cook.
- **Bonus 2**: Meditate for 10 mins. This bonus can only replace your motivational message. If you are unable to find a motivational message, take the time to meditate instead.

Afternoon Routine:

◈ **Document a beautiful moment**

> Find a priceless moment in the day that made you smile or made you happy. A priceless moment is not anything you can buy to make yourself happy. Example of a beautiful moment for me, when I hear birds chirping outside my window every morning, so I sit and listen while I drink my tea. I now believe they show up every morning to sing to me because they know I am in the moment with them and it makes me smile. Another example, the line was very long at the supermarket and I only had one thing and this wonderful lady allowed me to go ahead of her. This actually made my day because I was on a time crunch.

✻ **Bonus:** Meditate for 5 mins. I am including this meditation as an alternative if you cannot identify a beautiful moment, use your bonus to mark this section complete. I do recommend meditating every day for at least 5 mins even if you find a beautiful moment.

Evening Routine:

Please note that this section must be written in your journal nightly. I have given you extra space behind each page to complete this section of the transformational process. It is important to attack your negative thoughts until they stop attacking you. I recommend getting a journal specifically for this challenge.

◈ Document the negative emotions you encountered for the day.

It's ok to list them all and most importantly, to tell your mind how you want to react when faced with these emotions in the future. Give your mind clear instructions by reframing it into a positive sentence that will lead to a positive outcome.

Use the following format for this section:

1. What happened today that activated the negative emotion?
2. Why do you think you felt this way?
3. How do you want to react in the future?

Where suitable, reframe those thoughts into something positive. Well-being is experienced when you believe that you have the ability to access options that feel good to you for every challenge that you face.

Before Bed Routine:

◈ One thing that you are grateful for today? The grateful list can be as long as you like, but you must have one thing you are absolutely grateful for. It could be that you made it home safely, there was no traffic, you are healthy, you saw your parents today, you spent time with your friend. The grateful part is up to you. Let your soul lead this list. It will be pretty interesting to look and see how your grateful list has evolved over time. It's ok to be grateful for the same things every day. Please don't make this process difficult, it's not meant to make you think too hard. Everything you put in this journal should flow freely to you.

NOTE:

When you have completed a section, please use the square box on the left to place a checkmark. This represents you have completed the task.

REMEMBER: ONLY BEGIN WHEN YOU ARE READY TO DO THE WORK!

Living and Surviving are two different things.
~ Char Newell

| DAY 1 | **TO A NEW YOU** | DATE: .... |

Morning Routine: *Must be completed before you start your workday or leave the house.*

- ◈ Pray or repeat, "I am thankful for this beautiful day."
- ◈ Listen to a motivational message (10-30 mins long)
- ◈ Repeat a minimum of 3 positive affirmations over your life or set intentions for the day

◆ _____
_____
_____
_____
_____

◆ _____
_____
_____
_____
_____

◆ _____
_____
_____
_____
_____

✸ **Bonus:** Play relaxing, soothing, spa music while you shower and/or cook
✸ **Bonus 2**: Meditate for 10 mins. This bonus can only replace your motivational message.

Afternoon: *Must be completed by 2pm each day*

- ❖ Document a beautiful priceless moment

_____
_____
_____
_____

Bonus: Meditate for 5 mins

If you cannot identify a beautiful moment use this bonus and mark this section complete.

Evening Routine:

- ❖ Document the negative emotions you encountered for the day and reframe those thoughts

◆ _____
_____
_____
_____

Continue documenting your negative emotions on the next page.

Before Bed Routine:

- ❖ One thing that you are grateful for today?

◆ _____
_____

DAY 1 EMOTIONS

"There are three stages before the blessings; learning, developing, and the test."

DAY 1 EMOTIONS

DAY 1 EMOTIONS

DAY 2 | **TO A NEW YOU**   DATE: ....

Morning Routine: *Must be completed before you start your workday or leave the house.*

- ◈ Pray or repeat, "I am thankful for this beautiful day."
- ◈ Listen to a motivational message (10-30 mins long)
- ◈ Repeat a minimum of 3 positive affirmations over your life or set intentions for the day

- ◆ _____
  _____
  _____
  _____

- ◆ _____
  _____
  _____
  _____

- ◆ _____
  _____
  _____
  _____

✻ **Bonus:** Play relaxing, soothing, spa music while you shower and/or cook
✻ **Bonus 2**: Meditate for 10 mins. This bonus can only replace your motivational message.

Afternoon: *Must be completed by 2pm each day*

- ◈ Document a beautiful priceless moment

Bonus: Meditate for 5 mins

If you cannot identify a beautiful moment use this bonus and mark this section complete.

Evening Routine:

- ◈ Document the negative emotions you encountered for the day and reframe those thoughts

- ◆ _____
  _____
  _____
  _____

Continue documenting your negative emotions on the next page.

Before Bed Routine:

- ◈ One thing that you are grateful for today?

- ◆ _____
  _____

DAY 2 EMOTIONS

"Your weeds weren't meant to be pulled until they served their purpose".

DAY 2 EMOTIONS

DAY 2 EMOTIONS

DAY 3 | **TO A NEW YOU**   DATE: ....

Morning Routine: *Must be completed before you start your workday or leave the house.*

- ◈ Pray or repeat, "I am thankful for this beautiful day."
- ◈ Listen to a motivational message (10-30 mins long)
- ◈ Repeat a minimum of 3 positive affirmations over your life or set intentions for the day

- ◆ _____
  _____
  _____
  _____

- ◆ _____
  _____
  _____
  _____

- ◆ _____
  _____
  _____
  _____

✽ **Bonus:** Play relaxing, soothing, spa music while you shower and/or cook
✽ **Bonus 2**: Meditate for 10 mins. This bonus can only replace your motivational message.

Afternoon: *Must be completed by 2pm each day*

❖ Document a beautiful priceless moment

_____
_____
_____
_____
_____

Bonus: Meditate for 5 mins

If you cannot identify a beautiful moment use this bonus and mark this section complete.

Evening Routine:

❖ Document the negative emotions you encountered for the day and reframe those thoughts

◆ _____
_____
_____
_____

Continue documenting your negative emotions on the next page.

Before Bed Routine:

❖ One thing that you are grateful for today?

◆ _____
_____

DAY 3 EMOTIONS

"Your life is a classroom with a curriculum, and the exams are prepared lovingly by God."

DAY 3 EMOTIONS

DAY 3 EMOTIONS

DAY 4 | TO A NEW YOU

DATE: ....

Morning Routine: *Must be completed before you start your workday or leave the house.*

◈ Pray or repeat, "I am thankful for this beautiful day."

◈ Listen to a motivational message (10-30 mins long)

◈ Repeat a minimum of 3 positive affirmations over your life or set intentions for the day

◆ _____
_____
_____
_____
_____

◆ _____
_____
_____
_____
_____

◆ _____
_____
_____
_____
_____

✳ **Bonus:** Play relaxing, soothing, spa music while you shower and/or cook
✳ **Bonus 2**: Meditate for 10 mins. This bonus can only replace your motivational message.

Afternoon: *Must be completed by 2pm each day*

- ◈ Document a beautiful priceless moment

Bonus: Meditate for 5 mins

If you cannot identify a beautiful moment use this bonus and mark this section complete.

Evening Routine:

- ◈ Document the negative emotions you encountered for the day and reframe those thoughts

- ◆ _____
  _____
  _____
  _____

Continue documenting your negative emotions on the next page.

Before Bed Routine:

- ◈ One thing that you are grateful for today?

- ◆ _____
  _____

DAY 4 EMOTIONS

"Making excuses is a form of giving up."

DAY 4 EMOTIONS

DAY 4 EMOTIONS

| DAY 5 | **TO A NEW YOU** | DATE: .... |

Morning Routine: *Must be completed before you start your workday or leave the house.*

- Pray or repeat, "I am thankful for this beautiful day."
- Listen to a motivational message (10-30 mins long)
- Repeat a minimum of 3 positive affirmations over your life or set intentions for the day

◆ _____
_____
_____
_____
_____

◆ _____
_____
_____
_____
_____

◆ _____
_____
_____
_____
_____

✶ **Bonus:** Play relaxing, soothing, spa music while you shower and/or cook
✶ **Bonus 2**: Meditate for 10 mins. This bonus can only replace your motivational message.

Afternoon: *Must be completed by 2pm each day*

- ❖ Document a beautiful priceless moment

_____
_____
_____
_____

Bonus: Meditate for 5 mins

If you cannot identify a beautiful moment use this bonus and mark this section complete.

Evening Routine:

- ❖ Document the negative emotions you encountered for the day and reframe those thoughts

- ◆ _____
_____
_____
_____

Continue documenting your negative emotions on the next page.

Before Bed Routine:

- ❖ One thing that you are grateful for today?

- ◆ _____
_____

DAY 5 EMOTIONS

"Beauty is in the eye of the beholder."

DAY 5 EMOTIONS

DAY 5 EMOTIONS

| DAY 6 | **TO A NEW YOU** | DATE: .... |

Morning Routine: *Must be completed before you start your workday or leave the house.*

◈ Pray or repeat, "I am thankful for this beautiful day."

◈ Listen to a motivational message (10-30 mins long)

◈ Repeat a minimum of 3 positive affirmations over your life or set intentions for the day

◆ _____
_____
_____
_____
_____

◆ _____
_____
_____
_____
_____

◆ _____
_____
_____
_____
_____

✶ **Bonus:** Play relaxing, soothing, spa music while you shower and/or cook
✶ **Bonus 2**: Meditate for 10 mins. This bonus can only replace your motivational message.

Afternoon: *Must be completed by 2pm each day*

❖ Document a beautiful priceless moment

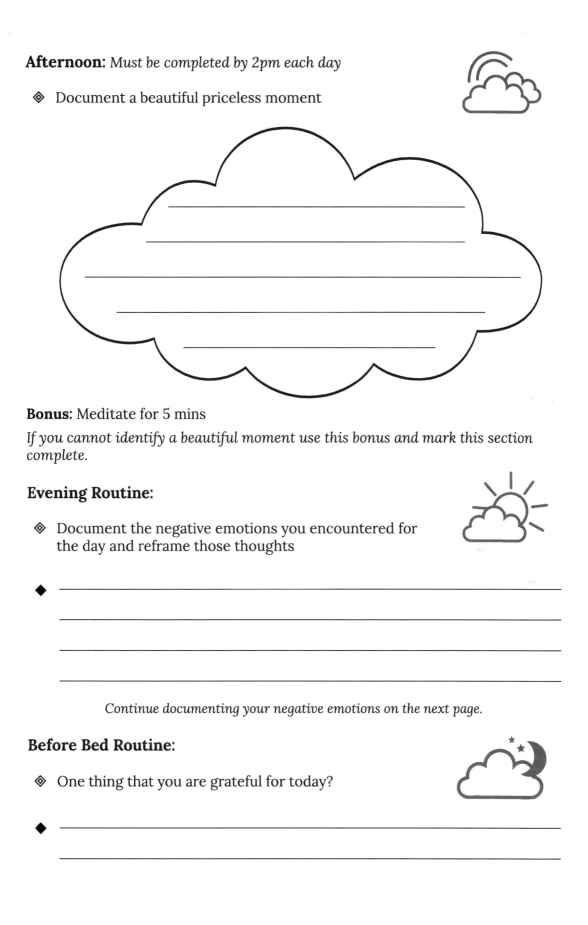

Bonus: Meditate for 5 mins

If you cannot identify a beautiful moment use this bonus and mark this section complete.

Evening Routine:

❖ Document the negative emotions you encountered for the day and reframe those thoughts

◆ _____
_____
_____
_____

Continue documenting your negative emotions on the next page.

Before Bed Routine:

❖ One thing that you are grateful for today?

◆ _____
_____

DAY 6 EMOTIONS

"You can quickly change the outcome of your story by applying a positive outlook and mindset to that negative situation."

DAY 6 EMOTIONS

DAY 6 EMOTIONS

DAY 7 | **TO A NEW YOU**   DATE: ....

Morning Routine: *Must be completed before you start your workday or leave the house.*

- ◈ Pray or repeat, "I am thankful for this beautiful day."
- ◈ Listen to a motivational message (10-30 mins long)
- ◈ Repeat a minimum of 3 positive affirmations over your life or set intentions for the day

- ◆ _____
  _____
  _____
  _____
  _____

- ◆ _____
  _____
  _____
  _____
  _____

- ◆ _____
  _____
  _____
  _____
  _____

✶ **Bonus:** Play relaxing, soothing, spa music while you shower and/or cook
✶ **Bonus 2**: Meditate for 10 mins. This bonus can only replace your motivational message.

Afternoon: *Must be completed by 2pm each day*

- ◈ Document a beautiful priceless moment

_____
_____
_____
_____

Bonus: Meditate for 5 mins

If you cannot identify a beautiful moment use this bonus and mark this section complete.

Evening Routine:

- ◈ Document the negative emotions you encountered for the day and reframe those thoughts

- ◆ _____
_____
_____
_____

Continue documenting your negative emotions on the next page.

Before Bed Routine:

- ◈ One thing that you are grateful for today?

- ◆ _____
_____

DAY 7 EMOTIONS

"Celebrate the small wins."

DAY 7 EMOTIONS

DAY 7 EMOTIONS

CONGRATULATIONS! YOU HAVE COMPLETED 7 DAYS

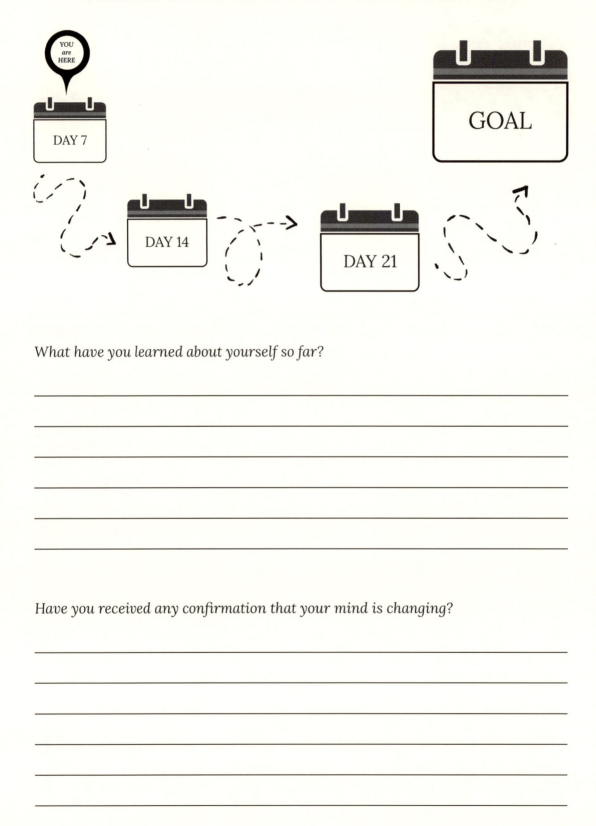

What have you learned about yourself so far?

_____
_____
_____
_____
_____
_____

Have you received any confirmation that your mind is changing?

_____
_____
_____
_____
_____
_____

| DAY 8 | **TO A NEW YOU** | DATE: .... |

Morning Routine: *Must be completed before you start your workday or leave the house.*

- Pray or repeat, "I am thankful for this beautiful day."
- Listen to a motivational message (10-30 mins long)
- Repeat a minimum of 3 positive affirmations over your life or set intentions for the day

◆ _____
_____
_____
_____
_____

◆ _____
_____
_____
_____
_____

◆ _____
_____
_____
_____
_____

✻ **Bonus:** Play relaxing, soothing, spa music while you shower and/or cook
✻ **Bonus 2**: Meditate for 10 mins. This bonus can only replace your motivational message.

Afternoon: *Must be completed by 2pm each day*

- ◈ Document a beautiful priceless moment

(cloud-shaped writing area with lines)

Bonus: Meditate for 5 mins

If you cannot identify a beautiful moment use this bonus and mark this section complete.

Evening Routine:

- ◈ Document the negative emotions you encountered for the day and reframe those thoughts

- ◆ _____
  _____
  _____
  _____

Continue documenting your negative emotions on the next page.

Before Bed Routine:

- ◈ One thing that you are grateful for today?

- ◆ _____
  _____

DAY 8 EMOTIONS

"Not everything in you was planted by you."

DAY 8 EMOTIONS

DAY 8 EMOTIONS

DAY 9 **TO A NEW YOU**   DATE: ....

Morning Routine: *Must be completed before you start your workday or leave the house.*

- ◈ Pray or repeat, "I am thankful for this beautiful day."
- ◈ Listen to a motivational message (10-30 mins long)
- ◈ Repeat a minimum of 3 positive affirmations over your life or set intentions for the day

◆ _____
_____
_____
_____
_____

◆ _____
_____
_____
_____
_____

◆ _____
_____
_____
_____
_____

✸ **Bonus:** Play relaxing, soothing, spa music while you shower and/or cook
✸ **Bonus 2:** Meditate for 10 mins. This bonus can only replace your motivational message.

Afternoon: *Must be completed by 2pm each day*

- ◈ Document a beautiful priceless moment

Bonus: Meditate for 5 mins

If you cannot identify a beautiful moment use this bonus and mark this section complete.

Evening Routine:

- ◈ Document the negative emotions you encountered for the day and reframe those thoughts

◆ _____

Continue documenting your negative emotions on the next page.

Before Bed Routine:

- ◈ One thing that you are grateful for today?

◆ _____

DAY 9 EMOTIONS

"Speak life into your soul."

DAY 9 EMOTIONS

DAY 9 EMOTIONS

DAY 10 | TO A NEW YOU

DATE: ....

Morning Routine: *Must be completed before you start your workday or leave the house.*

- ◈ Pray or repeat, "I am thankful for this beautiful day."
- ◈ Listen to a motivational message (10-30 mins long)
- ◈ Repeat a minimum of 3 positive affirmations over your life or set intentions for the day

- ◆ _____
  _____
  _____
  _____
  _____

- ◆ _____
  _____
  _____
  _____
  _____

- ◆ _____
  _____
  _____
  _____
  _____

✸ **Bonus:** Play relaxing, soothing, spa music while you shower and/or cook
✸ **Bonus 2:** Meditate for 10 mins. This bonus can only replace your motivational message.

Afternoon: *Must be completed by 2pm each day*

- ❖ Document a beautiful priceless moment

_____
_____
_____
_____

Bonus: Meditate for 5 mins

If you cannot identify a beautiful moment use this bonus and mark this section complete.

Evening Routine:

- ❖ Document the negative emotions you encountered for the day and reframe those thoughts

◆ _____
_____
_____
_____

Continue documenting your negative emotions on the next page.

Before Bed Routine:

- ❖ One thing that you are grateful for today?

◆ _____
_____

DAY 10 EMOTIONS

"Identifying your weaknesses is a form of self-love."

DAY 10 EMOTIONS

DAY 10 EMOTIONS

DAY 11 | TO A NEW YOU

DATE: ....

Morning Routine: *Must be completed before you start your workday or leave the house.*

- ◈ Pray or repeat, "I am thankful for this beautiful day."
- ◈ Listen to a motivational message (10-30 mins long)
- ◈ Repeat a minimum of 3 positive affirmations over your life or set intentions for the day

- ◆ _____
  _____
  _____
  _____
  _____

- ◆ _____
  _____
  _____
  _____
  _____

- ◆ _____
  _____
  _____
  _____
  _____

✶ **Bonus:** Play relaxing, soothing, spa music while you shower and/or cook
✶ **Bonus 2**: Meditate for 10 mins. This bonus can only replace your motivational message.

Afternoon: *Must be completed by 2pm each day*

- ◈ Document a beautiful priceless moment

Bonus: Meditate for 5 mins

If you cannot identify a beautiful moment use this bonus and mark this section complete.

Evening Routine:

- ◈ Document the negative emotions you encountered for the day and reframe those thoughts

◆ _____
_____
_____
_____

Continue documenting your negative emotions on the next page.

Before Bed Routine:

- ◈ One thing that you are grateful for today?

◆ _____
_____

DAY 11 EMOTIONS

"There are levels to your being."

DAY 11 EMOTIONS

DAY 11 EMOTIONS

DAY 12 | **TO A NEW YOU**   DATE: ....

Morning Routine: *Must be completed before you start your workday or leave the house.*

- Pray or repeat, "I am thankful for this beautiful day."
- Listen to a motivational message (10-30 mins long)
- Repeat a minimum of 3 positive affirmations over your life or set intentions for the day

- ◆ _____
  _____
  _____
  _____
  _____

- ◆ _____
  _____
  _____
  _____
  _____

- ◆ _____
  _____
  _____
  _____
  _____

✻ **Bonus:** Play relaxing, soothing, spa music while you shower and/or cook
✻ **Bonus 2:** Meditate for 10 mins. This bonus can only replace your motivational message.

Afternoon: *Must be completed by 2pm each day*

◈ Document a beautiful priceless moment

Bonus: Meditate for 5 mins

If you cannot identify a beautiful moment use this bonus and mark this section complete.

Evening Routine:

◈ Document the negative emotions you encountered for the day and reframe those thoughts

◆ _____
_____
_____
_____

Continue documenting your negative emotions on the next page.

Before Bed Routine:

◈ One thing that you are grateful for today?

◆ _____
_____

DAY 12 EMOTIONS

"Success in life requires discipline."

DAY 12 EMOTIONS

DAY 12 EMOTIONS

DAY 13 | **TO A NEW YOU**   DATE: ....

Morning Routine: *Must be completed before you start your workday or leave the house.*

- ◈ Pray or repeat, "I am thankful for this beautiful day."
- ◈ Listen to a motivational message (10-30 mins long)
- ◈ Repeat a minimum of 3 positive affirmations over your life or set intentions for the day

◆ _____
_____
_____
_____
_____

◆ _____
_____
_____
_____
_____

◆ _____
_____
_____
_____
_____

✳ **Bonus:** Play relaxing, soothing, spa music while you shower and/or cook
✳ **Bonus 2**: Meditate for 10 mins. This bonus can only replace your motivational message.

Afternoon: *Must be completed by 2pm each day*

◈ Document a beautiful priceless moment

_____
_____
_____
_____

Bonus: Meditate for 5 mins

If you cannot identify a beautiful moment use this bonus and mark this section complete.

Evening Routine:

◈ Document the negative emotions you encountered for the day and reframe those thoughts

◆ _____
_____
_____
_____

Continue documenting your negative emotions on the next page.

Before Bed Routine:

◈ One thing that you are grateful for today?

◆ _____
_____

DAY 13 EMOTIONS

"You can quickly change the outcome of your story by applying a positive outlook and mindset to that negative situation."

DAY 13 EMOTIONS

DAY 13 EMOTIONS

| DAY 14 | **TO A NEW YOU** | DATE: .... |

Morning Routine: *Must be completed before you start your workday or leave the house.*

- ◈ Pray or repeat, "I am thankful for this beautiful day."
- ◈ Listen to a motivational message (10-30 mins long)
- ◈ Repeat a minimum of 3 positive affirmations over your life or set intentions for the day

◆ _____
  _____
  _____
  _____
  _____

◆ _____
  _____
  _____
  _____
  _____

◆ _____
  _____
  _____
  _____
  _____

✱ **Bonus:** Play relaxing, soothing, spa music while you shower and/or cook
✱ **Bonus 2:** Meditate for 10 mins. This bonus can only replace your motivational message.

Afternoon: *Must be completed by 2pm each day*

- ❖ Document a beautiful priceless moment

_____
_____
_____
_____

Bonus: Meditate for 5 mins

If you cannot identify a beautiful moment use this bonus and mark this section complete.

Evening Routine:

- ❖ Document the negative emotions you encountered for the day and reframe those thoughts

- ◆ _____
  _____
  _____
  _____

Continue documenting your negative emotions on the next page.

Before Bed Routine:

- ❖ One thing that you are grateful for today?

- ◆ _____
  _____

DAY 14 EMOTIONS

"The trimming process requires you to give some things to get others."

DAY 14 EMOTIONS

DAY 14 EMOTIONS

CONGRATULATIONS! YOU HAVE COMPLETED 14 DAYS

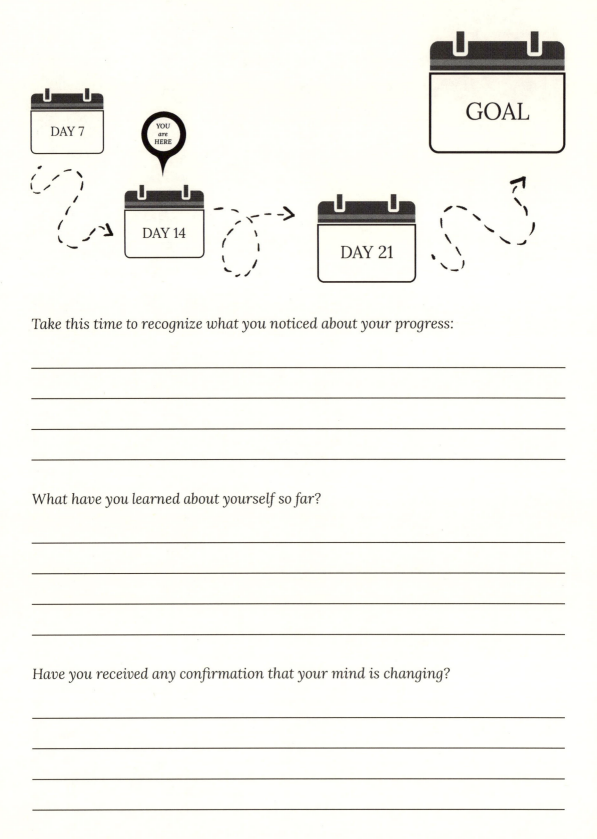

Take this time to recognize what you noticed about your progress:

_____
_____
_____
_____

What have you learned about yourself so far?

_____
_____
_____
_____

Have you received any confirmation that your mind is changing?

_____
_____
_____
_____

| DAY 15 | **TO A NEW YOU** | DATE: .... |

Morning Routine: *Must be completed before you start your workday or leave the house.*

- ◈ Pray or repeat, "I am thankful for this beautiful day."
- ◈ Listen to a motivational message (10-30 mins long)
- ◈ Repeat a minimum of 3 positive affirmations over your life or set intentions for the day

◆ _____
_____
_____
_____
_____

◆ _____
_____
_____
_____
_____

◆ _____
_____
_____
_____
_____

✶ **Bonus:** Play relaxing, soothing, spa music while you shower and/or cook
✶ **Bonus 2**: Meditate for 10 mins. This bonus can only replace your motivational message.

Afternoon: *Must be completed by 2pm each day*

◈ Document a beautiful priceless moment

Bonus: Meditate for 5 mins

If you cannot identify a beautiful moment use this bonus and mark this section complete.

Evening Routine:

◈ Document the negative emotions you encountered for the day and reframe those thoughts

◆ _____
_____
_____
_____

Continue documenting your negative emotions on the next page.

Before Bed Routine:

◈ One thing that you are grateful for today?

◆ _____
_____

DAY 15 EMOTIONS

"Become your own GPS, map out happiness and find good relationships."

DAY 15 EMOTIONS

DAY 15 EMOTIONS

DAY 16 | **TO A NEW YOU** | DATE: ....

Morning Routine: *Must be completed before you start your workday or leave the house.*

- Pray or repeat, "I am thankful for this beautiful day."
- Listen to a motivational message (10-30 mins long)
- Repeat a minimum of 3 positive affirmations over your life or set intentions for the day

◆ _____
_____
_____
_____
_____

◆ _____
_____
_____
_____
_____

◆ _____
_____
_____
_____
_____

✷ **Bonus:** Play relaxing, soothing, spa music while you shower and/or cook
✷ **Bonus 2**: Meditate for 10 mins. This bonus can only replace your motivational message.

Afternoon: *Must be completed by 2pm each day*

❖ Document a beautiful priceless moment

_____

Bonus: Meditate for 5 mins

If you cannot identify a beautiful moment use this bonus and mark this section complete.

Evening Routine:

❖ Document the negative emotions you encountered for the day and reframe those thoughts

◆ _____
_____
_____
_____

Continue documenting your negative emotions on the next page.

Before Bed Routine:

❖ One thing that you are grateful for today?

◆ _____
_____

DAY 16 EMOTIONS

"Your journey is unique to you."

DAY 16 EMOTIONS

DAY 16 EMOTIONS

YOU'RE HALFWAY THERE!!
Keep Going

Let's be honest, how are you feeling?

_____
_____
_____
_____
_____
_____
_____
_____
_____
_____
_____
_____
_____
_____
_____
_____
_____
_____
_____
_____
_____
_____
_____
_____
_____

DAY 17 | **TO A NEW YOU**   DATE: ....

Morning Routine: *Must be completed before you start your workday or leave the house.*

- ◈ Pray or repeat, "I am thankful for this beautiful day."
- ◈ Listen to a motivational message (10-30 mins long)
- ◈ Repeat a minimum of 3 positive affirmations over your life or set intentions for the day

- ◆ _____
  _____
  _____
  _____
  _____

- ◆ _____
  _____
  _____
  _____
  _____

- ◆ _____
  _____
  _____
  _____
  _____

✻ **Bonus:** Play relaxing, soothing, spa music while you shower and/or cook
✻ **Bonus 2**: Meditate for 10 mins. This bonus can only replace your motivational message.

Afternoon: *Must be completed by 2pm each day*

- ◈ Document a beautiful priceless moment

Bonus: Meditate for 5 mins

If you cannot identify a beautiful moment use this bonus and mark this section complete.

Evening Routine:

- ◈ Document the negative emotions you encountered for the day and reframe those thoughts

◆ _____
_____
_____
_____

Continue documenting your negative emotions on the next page.

Before Bed Routine:

- ◈ One thing that you are grateful for today?

◆ _____
_____

DAY 17 EMOTIONS

"Not everything planted in you was planted by you."

DAY 17 EMOTIONS

DAY 17 EMOTIONS

| DAY 18 | **TO A NEW YOU** | DATE: |

Morning Routine: *Must be completed before you start your workday or leave the house.*

- ◈ Pray or repeat, "I am thankful for this beautiful day."
- ◈ Listen to a motivational message (10-30 mins long)
- ◈ Repeat a minimum of 3 positive affirmations over your life or set intentions for the day

- ◆ _____
  _____
  _____
  _____

- ◆ _____
  _____
  _____
  _____

- ◆ _____
  _____
  _____
  _____

✻ **Bonus:** Play relaxing, soothing, spa music while you shower and/or cook
✻ **Bonus 2**: Meditate for 10 mins. This bonus can only replace your motivational message.

Afternoon: *Must be completed by 2pm each day*

- ❖ Document a beautiful priceless moment

_____
_____
_____
_____

Bonus: Meditate for 5 mins

If you cannot identify a beautiful moment use this bonus and mark this section complete.

Evening Routine:

- ❖ Document the negative emotions you encountered for the day and reframe those thoughts

◆ _____
_____
_____
_____

Continue documenting your negative emotions on the next page.

Before Bed Routine:

- ❖ One thing that you are grateful for today?

◆ _____
_____

DAY 18 EMOTIONS

"There are three stages before the blessings; learning, developing, and the test."

DAY 18 EMOTIONS

DAY 18 EMOTIONS

DAY 19 | **TO A NEW YOU**   DATE: ....

Morning Routine: *Must be completed before you start your workday or leave the house.*

- ◈ Pray or repeat, "I am thankful for this beautiful day."
- ◈ Listen to a motivational message (10-30 mins long)
- ◈ Repeat a minimum of 3 positive affirmations over your life or set intentions for the day

- ◆ _____
  _____
  _____
  _____
  _____

- ◆ _____
  _____
  _____
  _____
  _____

- ◆ _____
  _____
  _____
  _____
  _____

✻ **Bonus:** Play relaxing, soothing, spa music while you shower and/or cook
✻ **Bonus 2**: Meditate for 10 mins. This bonus can only replace your motivational message.

Afternoon: *Must be completed by 2pm each day*

- ◈ Document a beautiful priceless moment

_____
_____
_____
_____

Bonus: Meditate for 5 mins

If you cannot identify a beautiful moment use this bonus and mark this section complete.

Evening Routine:

- ◈ Document the negative emotions you encountered for the day and reframe those thoughts

◆ _____
_____
_____
_____

Continue documenting your negative emotions on the next page.

Before Bed Routine:

- ◈ One thing that you are grateful for today?

◆ _____
_____

DAY 19 EMOTIONS

"Meditate"

DAY 19 EMOTIONS

DAY 19 EMOTIONS

DAY 20 | **TO A NEW YOU**   DATE: ....

Morning Routine: *Must be completed before you start your workday or leave the house.*

- ◈ Pray or repeat, "I am thankful for this beautiful day."
- ◈ Listen to a motivational message (10-30 mins long)
- ◈ Repeat a minimum of 3 positive affirmations over your life or set intentions for the day

- ◆ _____
  _____
  _____
  _____
  _____

- ◆ _____
  _____
  _____
  _____
  _____

- ◆ _____
  _____
  _____
  _____
  _____

✳ **Bonus:** Play relaxing, soothing, spa music while you shower and/or cook
✳ **Bonus 2**: Meditate for 10 mins. This bonus can only replace your motivational message.

Afternoon: *Must be completed by 2pm each day*

❖ Document a beautiful priceless moment

Bonus: Meditate for 5 mins

If you cannot identify a beautiful moment use this bonus and mark this section complete.

Evening Routine:

❖ Document the negative emotions you encountered for the day and reframe those thoughts

◆ _____
_____
_____
_____

Continue documenting your negative emotions on the next page.

Before Bed Routine:

❖ One thing that you are grateful for today?

◆ _____
_____

DAY 20 EMOTIONS

"Don't lower your standards to feel successful."

DAY 20 EMOTIONS

DAY 20 EMOTIONS

| DAY 21 | **TO A NEW YOU** | DATE: .... |

Morning Routine: *Must be completed before you start your workday or leave the house.*

- ◈ Pray or repeat, "I am thankful for this beautiful day."
- ◈ Listen to a motivational message (10-30 mins long)
- ◈ Repeat a minimum of 3 positive affirmations over your life or set intentions for the day

◆ _____
_____
_____
_____
_____

◆ _____
_____
_____
_____
_____

◆ _____
_____
_____
_____
_____

✷ **Bonus:** Play relaxing, soothing, spa music while you shower and/or cook
✷ **Bonus 2**: Meditate for 10 mins. This bonus can only replace your motivational message.

Afternoon: *Must be completed by 2pm each day*

◈ Document a beautiful priceless moment

Bonus: Meditate for 5 mins

If you cannot identify a beautiful moment use this bonus and mark this section complete.

Evening Routine:

◈ Document the negative emotions you encountered for the day and reframe those thoughts

◆ _____

Continue documenting your negative emotions on the next page.

Before Bed Routine:

◈ One thing that you are grateful for today?

◆ _____

DAY 21 EMOTIONS

"You are starting to look beautiful, your soul is beginning to glow'"

DAY 21 EMOTIONS

DAY 21 EMOTIONS

IT'S TIME TO CELEBRATE! 21 DAYS COMPLETED

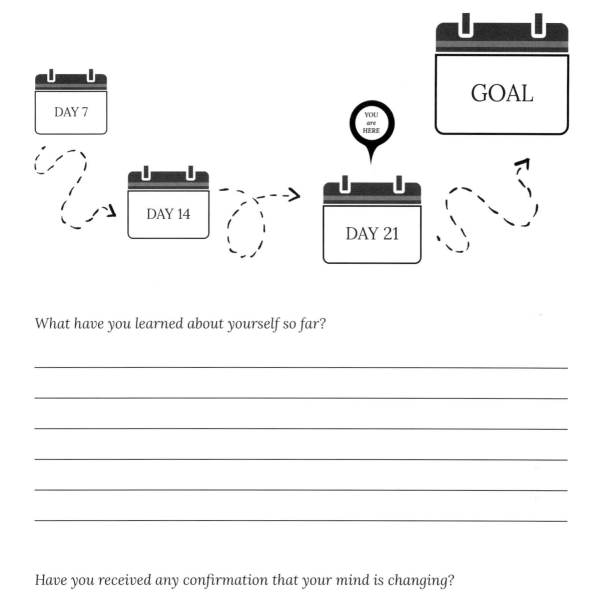

What have you learned about yourself so far?

_____
_____
_____
_____
_____
_____

Have you received any confirmation that your mind is changing?

_____
_____
_____
_____
_____
_____

| DAY 22 | **TO A NEW YOU** | DATE: ....

Morning Routine: *Must be completed before you start your workday or leave the house.*

- ◈ Pray or repeat, "I am thankful for this beautiful day."
- ◈ Listen to a motivational message (10-30 mins long)
- ◈ Repeat a minimum of 3 positive affirmations over your life or set intentions for the day

◆ _____
_____
_____
_____
_____

◆ _____
_____
_____
_____
_____

◆ _____
_____
_____
_____
_____

✶ **Bonus:** Play relaxing, soothing, spa music while you shower and/or cook
✶ **Bonus 2**: Meditate for 10 mins. This bonus can only replace your motivational message.

Afternoon: *Must be completed by 2pm each day*

◈ Document a beautiful priceless moment

_____
_____
_____
_____

Bonus: Meditate for 5 mins

If you cannot identify a beautiful moment use this bonus and mark this section complete.

Evening Routine:

◈ Document the negative emotions you encountered for the day and reframe those thoughts

◆ _____
_____
_____
_____

Continue documenting your negative emotions on the next page.

Before Bed Routine:

◈ One thing that you are grateful for today?

◆ _____
_____

DAY 22 EMOTIONS

"Your spiritual connection is a priority."

DAY 22 EMOTIONS

DAY 22 EMOTIONS

| DAY 23 | **TO A NEW YOU** | DATE: .... |

Morning Routine: *Must be completed before you start your workday or leave the house.*

◈ Pray or repeat, "I am thankful for this beautiful day."

◈ Listen to a motivational message (10-30 mins long)

◈ Repeat a minimum of 3 positive affirmations over your life or set intentions for the day

◆ _____
_____
_____
_____

◆ _____
_____
_____
_____

◆ _____
_____
_____
_____

✵ **Bonus:** Play relaxing, soothing, spa music while you shower and/or cook
✵ **Bonus 2**: Meditate for 10 mins. This bonus can only replace your motivational message.

Afternoon: *Must be completed by 2pm each day*

- ❖ Document a beautiful priceless moment

Bonus: Meditate for 5 mins

If you cannot identify a beautiful moment use this bonus and mark this section complete.

Evening Routine:

- ❖ Document the negative emotions you encountered for the day and reframe those thoughts

- ◆ _____

Continue documenting your negative emotions on the next page.

Before Bed Routine:

- ❖ One thing that you are grateful for today?

- ◆ _____

DAY 23 EMOTIONS

"Be in the moment."

DAY 23 EMOTIONS

DAY 23 EMOTIONS

DAY 24 | TO A NEW YOU

DATE: ....

Morning Routine: *Must be completed before you start your workday or leave the house.*

- ◈ Pray or repeat, "I am thankful for this beautiful day."
- ◈ Listen to a motivational message (10-30 mins long)
- ◈ Repeat a minimum of 3 positive affirmations over your life or set intentions for the day

◆ _____
_____
_____
_____
_____

◆ _____
_____
_____
_____
_____

◆ _____
_____
_____
_____
_____

✶ **Bonus:** Play relaxing, soothing, spa music while you shower and/or cook
✶ **Bonus 2**: Meditate for 10 mins. This bonus can only replace your motivational message.

Afternoon: *Must be completed by 2pm each day*

- Document a beautiful priceless moment

_____
_____
_____
_____

Bonus: Meditate for 5 mins

If you cannot identify a beautiful moment use this bonus and mark this section complete.

Evening Routine:

- Document the negative emotions you encountered for the day and reframe those thoughts

◆ _____
_____
_____
_____

Continue documenting your negative emotions on the next page.

Before Bed Routine:

- One thing that you are grateful for today?

◆ _____
_____

DAY 24 EMOTIONS

"You are operating at a higher level."

DAY 24 EMOTIONS

DAY 24 EMOTIONS

| DAY 25 | **TO A NEW YOU** | DATE: .... |

Morning Routine: *Must be completed before you start your workday or leave the house.*

◈ Pray or repeat, "I am thankful for this beautiful day."

◈ Listen to a motivational message (10-30 mins long)

◈ Repeat a minimum of 3 positive affirmations over your life or set intentions for the day

◆ _____
_____
_____
_____
_____

◆ _____
_____
_____
_____
_____

◆ _____
_____
_____
_____
_____

✻ **Bonus:** Play relaxing, soothing, spa music while you shower and/or cook
✻ **Bonus 2**: Meditate for 10 mins. This bonus can only replace your motivational message.

Afternoon: *Must be completed by 2pm each day*

◈ Document a beautiful priceless moment

Bonus: Meditate for 5 mins

If you cannot identify a beautiful moment use this bonus and mark this section complete.

Evening Routine:

◈ Document the negative emotions you encountered for the day and reframe those thoughts

◆ _____
_____
_____
_____

Continue documenting your negative emotions on the next page.

Before Bed Routine:

◈ One thing that you are grateful for today?

◆ _____
_____

DAY 25 EMOTIONS

"Believe you've got this, and you've got this"

DAY 25 EMOTIONS

DAY 25 EMOTIONS

DAY 26 | **TO A NEW YOU**   DATE: ....

Morning Routine: *Must be completed before you start your workday or leave the house.*

- ◈ Pray or repeat, "I am thankful for this beautiful day."
- ◈ Listen to a motivational message (10-30 mins long)
- ◈ Repeat a minimum of 3 positive affirmations over your life or set intentions for the day

◆ _____
_____
_____
_____
_____

◆ _____
_____
_____
_____
_____

◆ _____
_____
_____
_____
_____

✻ **Bonus:** Play relaxing, soothing, spa music while you shower and/or cook
✻ **Bonus 2**: Meditate for 10 mins. This bonus can only replace your motivational message.

Afternoon: *Must be completed by 2pm each day*

◈ Document a beautiful priceless moment

Bonus: Meditate for 5 mins

If you cannot identify a beautiful moment use this bonus and mark this section complete.

Evening Routine:

◈ Document the negative emotions you encountered for the day and reframe those thoughts

◆ _____
_____
_____
_____

Continue documenting your negative emotions on the next page.

Before Bed Routine:

◈ One thing that you are grateful for today?

◆ _____
_____

DAY 26 EMOTIONS

"Do things every day that makes you happy."

DAY 26 EMOTIONS

DAY 26 EMOTIONS

| DAY 27 | **TO A NEW YOU** | DATE: .... |

Morning Routine: *Must be completed before you start your workday or leave the house.*

- ❖ Pray or repeat, "I am thankful for this beautiful day."
- ❖ Listen to a motivational message (10-30 mins long)
- ❖ Repeat a minimum of 3 positive affirmations over your life or set intentions for the day

◆ _____
_____
_____
_____
_____

◆ _____
_____
_____
_____
_____

◆ _____
_____
_____
_____
_____

✸ **Bonus:** Play relaxing, soothing, spa music while you shower and/or cook
✸ **Bonus 2**: Meditate for 10 mins. This bonus can only replace your motivational message.

Afternoon: *Must be completed by 2pm each day*

◈ Document a beautiful priceless moment

_____
_____
_____
_____
_____

Bonus: Meditate for 5 mins

If you cannot identify a beautiful moment use this bonus and mark this section complete.

Evening Routine:

◈ Document the negative emotions you encountered for the day and reframe those thoughts

◆ _____
_____
_____
_____

Continue documenting your negative emotions on the next page.

Before Bed Routine:

◈ One thing that you are grateful for today?

◆ _____
_____

DAY 27 EMOTIONS

"Life is waiting on you to show up."

DAY 27 EMOTIONS

DAY 27 EMOTIONS

| DAY 28 | **TO A NEW YOU** | DATE: ....

Morning Routine: *Must be completed before you start your workday or leave the house.*

- ◈ Pray or repeat, "I am thankful for this beautiful day."
- ◈ Listen to a motivational message (10-30 mins long)
- ◈ Repeat a minimum of 3 positive affirmations over your life or set intentions for the day

- ◆ _____
  _____
  _____
  _____

- ◆ _____
  _____
  _____
  _____

- ◆ _____
  _____
  _____
  _____

✻ **Bonus:** Play relaxing, soothing, spa music while you shower and/or cook
✻ **Bonus 2**: Meditate for 10 mins. This bonus can only replace your motivational message.

Afternoon: *Must be completed by 2pm each day*

- ◈ Document a beautiful priceless moment

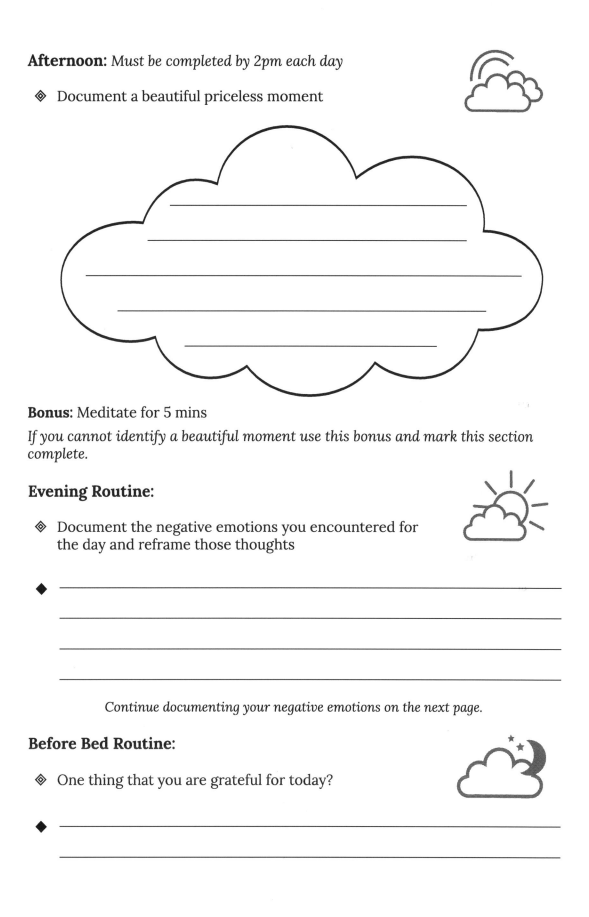

Bonus: Meditate for 5 mins

If you cannot identify a beautiful moment use this bonus and mark this section complete.

Evening Routine:

- ◈ Document the negative emotions you encountered for the day and reframe those thoughts

- ◆ _____
  _____
  _____
  _____

Continue documenting your negative emotions on the next page.

Before Bed Routine:

- ◈ One thing that you are grateful for today?

- ◆ _____
  _____

DAY 28 EMOTIONS

"Wake up expecting great things and great things will happen."

DAY 28 EMOTIONS

DAY 28 EMOTIONS

| DAY 29 | **TO A NEW YOU** | DATE: |

Morning Routine: *Must be completed before you start your workday or leave the house.*

- ◈ Pray or repeat, "I am thankful for this beautiful day."
- ◈ Listen to a motivational message (10-30 mins long)
- ◈ Repeat a minimum of 3 positive affirmations over your life or set intentions for the day

◆ _____
_____
_____
_____
_____

◆ _____
_____
_____
_____
_____

◆ _____
_____
_____
_____
_____

✸ **Bonus:** Play relaxing, soothing, spa music while you shower and/or cook
✸ **Bonus 2**: Meditate for 10 mins. This bonus can only replace your motivational message.

Afternoon: *Must be completed by 2pm each day*

◈ Document a beautiful priceless moment

Bonus: Meditate for 5 mins

If you cannot identify a beautiful moment use this bonus and mark this section complete.

Evening Routine:

◈ Document the negative emotions you encountered for the day and reframe those thoughts

◆ _____
_____
_____
_____

Continue documenting your negative emotions on the next page.

Before Bed Routine:

◈ One thing that you are grateful for today?

◆ _____
_____

DAY 29 EMOTIONS

"Self-awareness is key."

DAY 29 EMOTIONS

DAY 29 EMOTIONS

| DAY 30 | **TO A NEW YOU** | DATE: .... |

Morning Routine: *Must be completed before you start your workday or leave the house.*

- ◈ Pray or repeat, "I am thankful for this beautiful day."
- ◈ Listen to a motivational message (10-30 mins long)
- ◈ Repeat a minimum of 3 positive affirmations over your life or set intentions for the day

◆ _____
_____
_____
_____
_____

◆ _____
_____
_____
_____
_____

◆ _____
_____
_____
_____
_____

✱ **Bonus:** Play relaxing, soothing, spa music while you shower and/or cook
✱ **Bonus 2**: Meditate for 10 mins. This bonus can only replace your motivational message.

Afternoon: *Must be completed by 2pm each day*

- ◈ Document a beautiful priceless moment

Bonus: Meditate for 5 mins

If you cannot identify a beautiful moment use this bonus and mark this section complete.

Evening Routine:

- ◈ Document the negative emotions you encountered for the day and reframe those thoughts

- ◆ _____

Continue documenting your negative emotions on the next page.

Before Bed Routine:

- ◈ One thing that you are grateful for today?

- ◆ _____

DAY 30 EMOTIONS

"Always recognize and embrace the process before the blessings."

DAY 30 EMOTIONS

DAY 30 EMOTIONS

MISSION ACCOMPLISHED!

Dear Life Warriors,

You did it! There is no way your mind should be the same. It will take some time to really master positive thinking, so I encourage you to keep going. I have added some extra blank pages for you to do so. Try to do this for another 30 days, and after that, I recommend journaling at least 3 times a week. The purpose of journaling is to have honest conversations with yourself and to recognize negative thought patterns. I also use journaling to let my intentions be known to God, so he can guide me in the right direction. Journaling is a form of self-care, so do this as often as possible because your true self lies within the pages of your journal.

I love you dearly,
Char Newell

BONUS DAY TO A NEW YOU

DATE: ....

Morning Routine: *Must be completed before you start your workday or leave the house.*

- ◈ Pray or repeat, "I am thankful for this beautiful day."
- ◈ Listen to a motivational message (10-30 mins long)
- ◈ Repeat a minimum of 3 positive affirmations over your life or set intentions for the day

◆ _____
_____
_____
_____
_____

◆ _____
_____
_____
_____
_____

◆ _____
_____
_____
_____
_____

✱ **Bonus:** Play relaxing, soothing, spa music while you shower and/or cook
✱ **Bonus 2:** Meditate for 10 mins. This bonus can only replace your motivational message.

Afternoon: *Must be completed by 2pm each day*

- ❖ Document a beautiful priceless moment

_____
_____
_____
_____

Bonus: Meditate for 5 mins

If you cannot identify a beautiful moment use this bonus and mark this section complete.

Evening Routine:

- ❖ Document the negative emotions you encountered for the day and reframe those thoughts

◆ _____
_____
_____
_____

Continue documenting your negative emotions on the next page.

Before Bed Routine:

- ❖ One thing that you are grateful for today?

◆ _____
_____

BONUS DAY EMOTIONS

BONUS DAY EMOTIONS

BONUS DAY EMOTIONS

DATE: ....

DATE: ....

DATE: ....

DATE: ....

DATE: ....

DATE: ....

DATE: ....

DATE: ....

DATE:

DATE: ....

DATE: ....

DATE: ....

DATE: ....

DATE: ....

DATE: ....

DATE: ....

DATE: ....

DATE: ....

DATE: ....

DATE: ....

DATE:

DATE: ....

DATE: ....

DATE: ....

DATE: ....

DATE: ....

DATE: ....

DATE: ....

DATE: ....

DATE: ....

About Char Newell

EMPOWERING employees and SEALING the void between them and upper management for over a DECADE... Char comes with a verified plan of attack, and a deep-rooted history in the areas of mergers and acquisitions, leadership development, culture transformation, change management, building organization capability and human capital process. Mix it all together for a uniquely effective holistic approach to corporate health that will stand the test of time! Sprinkle in her flair, drive, and a diverse healthcare background, and Char has made herself one of the most requested corporate life coaches around. She has led hundreds of high-volume mergers and successfully transformed broken cultures, resulting in a lower turnover and an increase in revenue for her clients! Char's vast pool of experience lives in healthcare industries on a national scale, such as: Behavioral Health, Homecare, Hospitals, Healthcare Management Services, Assisted Living Facilities and Medical Groups. She utilized the invaluable insight gained from attaining her Master of Industrial and Labor Relations from Zicklin School of Business at Baruch College and her bachelor's in marketing from CUNY, York College, to march forward and crush her goals.

Refusing to slow down, Char's innovative strategies landed her in the circles of top senior- level HR Executives with an invite-only spot on the Elite Forbes HR Council. Her work was recognized by the Young Gifted & Black Entrepreneurial Awards and she was honored with the Professional Services Award for Strategic Vision & Innovation in Human Resources! And that isn't the only way that Char is making waves in the HR arena, she packs an even bigger punch by mastering her discipline and attaining certifications for: Certified Corporate Life Coach (CCLC), Certified Relationship Consultant (CRC), Certified Holistic Health & Wellness Practitioner (CHWP), and last but definitely not least, Strategic Human Resources Business Partner (sHRBP).

With her unstoppable attitude, Char decided to magnify her growing knowledge in leadership development and human resources by starting Your Healthy Reality (YHR). This is an Management Consulting Agency dedicated to providing corporate life coaching services that helps businesses align their people strategy to the business strategy and fast-tracking professionals to paths of success while enabling organizations to achieve corporate health. She brightens up the airwaves with a delectable podcast that will keep listeners coming back for more, offering an exclusive perspective into a world of healthy relationships in the workplace, and how it ties in closely to a healthy mind. Her work in the field of Human Resources and in the community earned her the Certificate of Congressional Recognition from Congresswoman Yvette Clark!

"It's not just about running a successful business, it's about changing lives. We are dedicated to serving people by educating, empowering, motivating and giving hope."
– Char Newell.

Her mission
To educate, empower, motivate, & give hope to many.

Books by Char Newell
The Yellow Weed: How to Recognize & Embrace the Process Before the Blessings

www.yourhealthyreality.com | info@yourhealthyreality.com | IG: @boszilla @_yourhealthyreality

Made in the USA
Monee, IL
14 February 2022

05830724-f315-4f78-a886-efa7f812520fR01